CONT.

CONT.

Amy Evans

Shearsman Books

First published in the United Kingdom in 2015 by
Shearsman Books
50 Westons Hill Drive
Emersons Green
BRISTOL
BS16 7DF

Shearsman Books Ltd Registered Office
30–31 St. James Place, Mangotsfield, Bristol BS16 9JB
(this address not for correspondence)

www.shearsman.com

ISBN 978-1-84861-454-3

CONT.

husk y voiced   she
amid man(l)y   not/es
and   t/ones

collected,   *not per*
turbed   *or dis*:
tracted—

                      in trea/sure

tro(u)vé
    o(u)vert,   fineds

Echo—   *a nymph*
who was spurned   *by Narcissus*
and ~~pined away~~
~~until only~~   *—*
her voice   *remained*

who takes

To

Tr(ANS)
        s l*it*
            err ation

&

Erat umm:

raised, I browse

EX/panding   via
   /change   despite
   /pound

P. [T.] **S.** [D.]

shell   shock ed, she

de   live errs

after   much

lab   our,

bore (n.)   to death

l oosing   sp. each,

m out h   sh(o)uts

  OUT

over (the)   dose

and prop(ertie)s   co(a)st

lives, hive

                    off the rest
Inc. case it works

I will s/pend   my life
(up) on   [with]

you (rs)
                    ⁓
                    nec(essary) romance

payn packet each month
record (s) losses: are you g /one? I

have lost
                      my balance

-sheet is red
               marriage has
doubly
s tain (t)ed   all
I k new

             I do

n't vow,   n/either
publicly   n/or
sacredly   as I

have
lost my faith

             in all of you

hear t   £s

```
pulse-ugly    h ours
tick          and        tock boxes
that are not             little
and           are        now
```

comes *crash*   ing

occupy,   un *usually*
un   *invited*

          undergo
serious   Dam(n)
AGE

Yes, I am   f illed with rAge,

waving   & (dr)owning

a tendency to   *curl in a person*

              's h h h   *air*

vent   ing   with [*out* {*off*}]

con   *sequence*

un   able Two   S—TO—P—

        Per,
        Per,

            so(o)n . . .

Content   s:

s p*i*n   *ster* s

              mourning

              after

the   pill

faculties

laid   (b)are on
kitch en   (t)able as desk

tHis One will tell

a sTory, T AXiomatically

h*OW* [*E*]

APR is the T AXing month =
letter box m*out*hs

numb ers
IN poor VOICE

wHer e:

g\ate   Left   a/jar

off   ©   ENTER

, Miss   hap(p)en

Seaking   to rescue

self   with correctly

[from *cor*   and *regere*]

puckered   lips

                                                <   *emboushore*

May days:
when   s inking

there are   ap/proved sounds
sum   un/natural

dis Content   with what is contained
(*in a vessel,*   *book, law etc.*)

La [6 out of every 8] meant that

while water [4   5ths] is
                      common s + *represents*

flow of space
people   don't float

between   borders

                      nor in accordance

with stock   market
                                        ~   buoyancy

Triton   g rows
callus

seek   *wh*ence

shuns (clo)sure, eve

n   w hen

f allow *left*   *unSewn*

for a   .   *to re: sTore—*

st itches language, rig/gles

setting   s(n.)ail

s}hell}ed   animality

shhhh   : own

Silence   profits the

$lender

berried under

-tow   ≈ I Will

not be $

wept   a way

weighed   down,

fur ther,   *too*

wry(s)   (im)material,

gr owing   Her

own

s

       kin

To B C   Shell s

ever(y)   wear

Blowing   of/f the resCue

good(s)   for tune,   having

once,   twice, per Cystantly

B eached

To Be :   . . .

Con*t*ch / us

that all   she/ll   tell s — is

instrument all in   —

emerge nce   , , , sea

                     from B low   : horns'

notes dis cover   *spyre*al   dote *up*on b/ones

                          Be fore air   *A long*   ,

accompanied song   *for A*   *solo*

                               voice

www.ingramcontent.com/pod-product-compliance
Lightning Source LLC
Chambersburg PA
CBHW021947040426
42448CB00008B/1278